W9-BKN-538

FERRETS
AS A NEW PET

GREG OVECHKA

CONTENTS

Photographs by Glen S. Axelrod, Bonnie Buys, courtesy of Fabulous Ferrets, Isabelle Francais, Jan Hirschorn.

1995 edition

Distributed in the UNITED STATES to the Pet Trade by T.F.H. Publications, Inc., One T.F.H. Plaza, Neptune City, NJ 07753; distributed in the UNITED STATES to the Bookstore and Library Trade by National Book Network, Inc. 4720 Boston Way, Lanham MD 20706; in CANADA to the Pet Trade by H & L Pet Supplies Inc., 27 Kingston Crescent, Kitchener, Ontario N2B 2T6; Rolf C. Hagen Ltd., 3225 Sartelon Street, Montreal 382 Quebec; in CANADA to the Book Trade by Vanwell Publishing Ltd., 1 Northrup Crescent, St. Catharines, Ontario L2M 6P5 ; in ENGLAND by T.F.H. Publications, PO Box 15, Waterlooville PO7 6BQ; in AUSTRALIA AND THE SOUTH PACIFIC by T.F.H. (Australia), Pty. Ltd., Box 149, Brookvale 2100 N.S.W., Australia; in NEW ZEALAND by Brooklands Aquarium Ltd. 5 McGiven Drive, New Plymouth, RD1 New Zealand; in Japan by T.F.H. Publications, Japan—Jiro Tsuda, 10-12-3 Ohjidai, Sakura, Chiba 285, Japan; in SOUTH AFRICA by Lopis (Pty) Ltd., P.O. Box 39127, Booysens, 2016, Johannesburg, South Africa. Published by T.F.H. Publications, Inc.
MANUFACTURED IN THE UNITED STATES OF AMERICA
BY T.F.H. PUBLICATIONS, INC.

Introduction

The inclusion of any pet into a household can and will have a lifelong impact on that household. Ferrets, which are

entertainment. Ferrets are real hams: they pose for pictures; they play hide-and-seek; they go up and down the stairs like

Most ferrets are natural hams for friends, family, fellow ferrets, and photographs.

becoming increasingly popular pets, can provide tremendous enjoyment without tremendous sacrifice. In exchange for food, water, shelter, protection, and love, the ferret owner can expect companionship and hours of entertainment. Yes,

slinky toys; they even have their own toys, like balloons and baby pacifiers. As Jackie Gleason might have said, "They're a regular riot!"

When you're thinking about getting a ferret, you should keep certain things in mind. First of

Choosing one particular ferret from a litter may not be easy. Take your time in watching them at play to get an idea of their individual personalities.

all, ferrets are really no different than any other pets in that you, the pet owner, must be willing to assume certain responsibilities. You must be willing to provide your pet with the right kind of food, necessary health care, and clean surroundings. And if you travel a lot, or if you're not home very often, maybe you should consider the fact that ferrets, like most other pets, need to have you home at least once in a while. Few pets appreciate being left alone all the time. Then too, medical costs—for descenting, altering, vaccines—though not exorbitant, should also be taken into account.

The temptation to buy that cute little animal in the pet store window may be great, but unless you're prepared to take on all the obligations of being a pet owner, perhaps it's not the best thing to do—for you or for the animal.

It might also be a good idea for the prospective ferret owner to visit someone who already has a ferret. You should know what ferrets are like before you buy them. There are unique responsibilities involved in owning a ferret. You will have to, for one thing, ferret-proof your house. Ferrets like to get into and under things. Their slinky bodies and natural

Most ferrets are too curious to be afraid of new acquaintances and situations.

curiosity get them under refrigerators and stoves—and even under some doors.

A person thinking about acquiring a ferret should also know that ferrets, unlike dogs and cats, have a certain musky odor. Even ferrets that have been descented will still emit this odor. You will probably have to bathe the ferret from time to time. Do you have the time to do this? A person getting a ferret for the first time shouldn't wait until he or she has brought the animal home to find out all these things.

Now, after having said all this, if you would like to join the three million or so estimated ferret owners representing a ferret population of four to five million in the United States today, here are some things that you should think about before you get your first pet ferret.

BUYING A FERRET

Should you get a male or a female ferret? One ferret or two? How about a group of ferrets? Adult or kit? What color? Sable—the one with the bandit-mask that looks like a raccoon? An albino ferret? A silver ferret? Of course, a lot of this will depend on personal preference. But whatever you decide, make sure that you get a healthy ferret from a reputable person—whether the person is a local pet store owner or a ferret breeder.

Male and female ferrets need about the same amount of space and care, although neutering the male will be less expensive. They are equally hardy. While the male is bigger than the female, the sexes do not differ greatly in behavior—unless they are in heat! Ferrets all have their own individual personalities; their sex and/or color does not predetermine what they will be like as individual pets in your home.

As mentioned, male ferrets are larger than female ferrets—about twice their size, in fact. Male ferrets will range from three to five pounds and grow up to be about 17 inches in length, not including the tail.

Males also have broader faces, compared with the female's more pointed face. The male ferret that has been altered and descented will give off less of an odor than a male ferret which hasn't had this surgery. The female ferret, however, has the mildest odor. And all these surgical alterations are highly recommended for the domestic ferret. In the case of the female ferret, you, as a ferret owner, must—and this is *very important* to remember—have her spayed, unless she is being bred, before she goes into heat. If you don't see that this is

Male ferrets have broad faces, while those of the females are more pointed.

done, the female ferret will very likely develop a serious disease—aplastic anemia—which could cause her death.

What about selecting a ferret? What are some things to look for when you are in the market for a pet ferret? Many people would say that it's a matter of common sense to insist on finding an animal that looks alert and acts frisky. If you are like most people, you probably will not want an animal that looks lethargic and unresponsive. But then again, there are people who may cotton to that furry little guy in the back of the cage who looks so forlorn. But don't confuse health with personality. It's probably better for everyone if you see that the animal's nose isn't runny, or his eyes aren't too watery.

It is not absolutely necessary, as perhaps some pet dealers would have their customers believe, that ferrets be bought two and three at a time, or that they all be from the same litter. But you might consider the idea of getting two ferrets, instead of having an "only ferret." By doing this, you will be providing each ferret with a friend and companion. And when you are not there, the ferret won't be left alone.

Exactly where should one go to get a ferret? Again, a good thing might be to call someone

Healthy ferrets are active, playful creatures with unbridled curiosity about the world around them. A lethargic ferret is a sick ferret.

When visiting the pet shop or breeder, look around at the surroundings. If they are clean and well maintained, it is likely that the animals themselves are healthy.

who already has one. Ask if he is pleased with the ferret. Has it been healthy? If so, ask where he got it. Word of mouth is often a useful way of finding the best way to get all kinds of things, including ferrets.

On the more technical side, you might also want to try to find out when—at what age—the ferret you are thinking about bringing home was altered and/or descented. Some are being altered and descented when they are too young. The ferret can be harmed by this kind of surgery at too tender an age.

There have also been cases reported where ferrets, because of their young age or incorrect procedures, were not successfully operated on.

It might be more convenient, and you may even save a few dollars, to buy a ferret that has already been altered and descented. After all, you yourself would have to spend the time and money to find the veterinarian and have the surgery performed. However, it might be a good idea to do this. It could be a little more expensive, but it could make a big difference in the long-term health of your ferret. You could wind up with a much healthier pet if you take this kind of personal interest in this very important medical care.

But whatever you do and wherever you go, make sure that you know the reputation of the place where you are purchasing your ferret. If it's a pet store, look around it for a little while, and ask yourself, "Does it look clean? Are the sales people well-informed? Do they know anything about ferrets? Do they seem to care enough about the animals (and yours in particular)?"

You have the right to ask all kinds of questions. Those ferrets didn't just appear in that pet store. Someone raised them. Where did the ferrets come from? If neutered and descented, at what age? These operations should not be performed until the ferret—male or female—is at least six months of age. Yet some dealers, responding to the consumer demand for convenience at all costs, are selling ferrets which have been operated on at a very early age. If this isn't the way that you think an animal should be treated, you could request young ferrets that haven't yet gone under the surgeon's knife.

Or you could go directly to a ferret breeder. If you do, look at the hutches. Are the breeding conditions sanitary? You might even get to see the parents of the kit. How do they look?

In any case, be sure that the person who is selling you the ferret or ferrets is reputable—and cares about ferrets.

PREPARING FOR THE FERRET'S ARRIVAL

It will be a lot easier for you if you go shopping

Before bringing your new pet(s) home, pick up some safe toys at the pet shop.

before you bring home your first pet ferret. Your shopping list for your new pet should include a litter pan, along with enough litter. Most commercial cat litter pans and commercial brands of litter will be fine. Have food dishes ready. Ferrets like to move their food dishes around, so you might want to find some kind of weighted

especially on a warm, summer day. Ferrets need plenty of fresh drinking water. A vitamin supplement and a vitamin dropper will also be useful.

You will probably be bathing the ferret regularly, so you will need a gentle, tearless baby shampoo, and maybe a gentle conditioner. For clipping the ferret's nails, you will need a

It is imperative that you ferret-proof your home—blocking all openings and securing all appliances that might tempt your ferret.

food dish. Have some good, high protein dry cat food in the house—ferrets are always hungry. It will be useful to have a water bottle, or maybe two—one to put in the ferret's cage, and the other to take with you, if you are taking the ferrets out,

nail clipper—the kind used by people will do.

Other items that you should have ready for the ferret's arrival might include a comb and brush, a collar and identification tag, a leash and a harness.

Purchase a cage for your pet(s). A cage is a place for rest, relaxation, and security for the ferret.

While you will not be using a cage as a jail for your ferret, you will want to have some kind of cage in your home in order to help the animal get used to his new surroundings. By giving him a small place of his own to start out in, you will help him get settled. A new home with new people and new sounds can be frightening to a new pet. The cage can be a secure place for those first few days or weeks. It should be equipped with a water bottle, litter pan, and some comfortable, soft bedding. You might also, if there is room, put in a tissue box for the ferret to curl up in.

Handling Ferrets

"You have to handle them! You have to handle the ferret!" That's some of the best advice that a new owner can get. One impression—that these animals should be in cages for their entire lives.

Ferrets are sociable,

Pet ferrets should be handled by the breeder as soon as they are weaned. This way they are accustomed to people before they go to their new homes.

of the biggest mistakes, if not *the* biggest, that new ferret owners make is not handling the pet. Some people seem to have the wrong idea about ferrets. They seem to think of them as critters akin to the hamster, guinea pig, white mice or other animals. They seem to have the impression—and it's the *wrong* domesticated, playful, affectionate, gentle animals. They need to be held and treated kindly.

Treat the ferret in a gentle manner. Talk to it in a soothing, quiet tone of voice. Breeders, pet store owners, and long-time ferret owners agree that the ferret that has been treated with

Ferrets, like people, occasionally have an itch to scratch. If, however, your pet scratches incessantly, take him to the vet.

love and kindness is going to make the better pet.

Said one ferret breeder, "I think a lot depends on the kind of handling they get when they're young; that seems to make the biggest difference. And that's what we try to do here. We've seen a lot of cases where people were selling ferrets that had been caged until someone brought them home. By that time, they were wild, and maybe even a little dangerous. Once the kits are weaned, at about four weeks, we take them into the house, set up cages, and handle them all the time. Then the babies are calmer and more tame. As ferret breeders, we feel that it is our responsibility to do this before we give them to someone else to take to their home. When we started out as breeders, that's what we decided our philosophy of breeding ferrets would be."

DON'T LET YOUR FERRET GO OUTSIDE ALONE

Ferrets are very dependent on people. The chances of one surviving in the wilds, or even in a suburban development, are not good. So don't open the back door and let your ferrets go outside in the yard as you would your cat. They could get lost outdoors, which could be a disaster. And if your pet has the misfortune to meet up with a bigger and meaner animal, it could even be a bigger disaster! Ferrets shouldn't be included in the same category (or backyard) as raccoons, foxes, and possums, and other animals technically defined as "wild animals." With the exception of its nearly extinct cousin, the black-footed ferret, ferret populations do not exist anywhere in the wild in the United States.

While you certainly don't ever want to let your ferret go outside unattended, there will probably be times when you will want to take him out for a walk and give him some fresh air. If you are taking your animal out for a walk, put a collar on him, along with a leash.

You might also want to do what many cat owners do: attach to the ferret's collar a small identification tag that has your name, address, and telephone number on it. This way, if your ferret ever does get loose, your neighbors will realize that it is a *domestic* pet that belongs to someone, not some wild animal. By putting an I.D. collar on your ferret, you will also be increasing your chances of getting your animal returned to you if he/she ever does get lost.

Never let your ferret outside unattended, and do not neglect to get him an I.D. collar and tag. Many owners take their pets for walks only with a leash attached to the collar.

Food for Ferrets

Pet ferrets can enjoy and thrive on a chow formulated just for them. For variety, some ferret owners also supplement this basic diet with a can of cat food every few days.

In additon to providing good nutrition, ferret chow has other benefits. It can be left out without spoiling or looking unappetizing. It is also good for the ferret's teeth and gums. And it

Silver mink, a member of the family Mustelidae, just like the domestic ferret. Some owners provide their pet ferrets with mink food when it is available.

can be cheaper than canned or moist food. You might also want to add a vitamin supplement to your ferret's diet.

Remember that a bowl or a bottle of fresh, clean drinking water should be available.

For those who read the fine print on packaged food, there's protein and then there's protein. By this we mean that ferrets perform much better on a diet containing a high percentage of *animal protein*. Many dry foods list on the package only the protein content; this could be largely *vegetable protein*, depending on the brand. Sometimes it's difficult to find out which protein is being served. Generally, you shouldn't skimp and buy cheap food

The bulk of your pet's diet should be dry chow formulated just for ferrets. If you are unsure about how much to feed your ferret, check with a vet. Photo courtesy Marshall Pet Products.

brands; they probably have less of the animal protein.

Although they are classified as carnivores, ferrets don't

A good diet—well-balanced and varied—should help to keep your ferret trim and active.

15

really need fresh meat, but a few table scraps here and there won't hurt them. Ferrets may also be given fresh fruit and vegetables, depending on their individual taste buds. Some may like cucumbers, while others may give anything for a blueberry.

A good, healthy diet will keep your ferret happy and playful throughout his life.

Snacks? These animals love snacks. But treats should be given only once in a while, and in small portions. Ferrets, for example, like ice cream. We've even seen one put away a Snickers Bar, peanuts and all.

Never give your ferret chicken or turkey bones; these can splinter and get caught in your pet's throat and intestinal tract.

Milk? Water—rather than milk—should be the drink of ferrets. Milk can be given in moderation, depending on whether or not your ferret has a tolerance

for it; it has been known to cause stomach upsets. If your ferret drinks milk and it causes diarrhea, stop giving it. Perhaps some time in the future, you could also try diluting the milk with a little water.

Young kits can be fed ferret food that has been mixed with water to soften it. The ferret grows quickly in its first few months and should have food and plenty of fresh, drinking water readily available. As the ferret starts growing to its normal size, watch his weight by restricting and monitoring the food intake.

Kits begin to show an interest in solid food in about three weeks, but they do not eat solid food exclusively until they are four or five weeks of age. Their body weight will increase gradually up to that point. Then it will increase sharply until adult weight is attained.

What about the older ferret? A ferret that is well cared for can live a long life—an average of eight to ten years. But the older ferret might need some extra care. It can develop tooth problems, for one thing. If your pet seems to have trouble chewing food, add some water to the food to soften it. The older ferret, like other domestic animals, can also develop digestive problems. When your ferret gets to be about seven or eight years old, consider putting one-half a teaspoon of vegetable oil in its food once a day to help maintain its digestive regularity. Vegetable oil also helps keep the ferret's coat in good

"Kits begin to show an interest in solid food in about three weeks, but they do not eat solid food exclusively until they are four or five weeks of age."

A trio of ferret kits. When feeding multiple ferrets, be sure each is getting enough to eat.

condition.

One last bit of advice: ferrets like to hide their food. Sometimes under your sofa! This should motivate you to clean up after the ferret has eaten one of his usual two daily meals.

And again, always leave out enough fresh drinking water for the animal—especially in the warm weather.

Snacks are fine if they are given as special treats or as rewards during trick training. Don't overfeed your ferrets.

Bathing and Grooming

Although ferrets may wash themselves occasionally, it's a good idea to give them a bath to

thing for you to do is to keep an eye on them when they're in the water.

Below: Like many other small mammals, some ferrets can be prone to coat problems, including dryness and itchiness. Pet shops carry ferret grooming products that can help to provide relief. Photo courtesy Four Paws.

Although this fellow doesn't look too happy, ferret bathing is a must. Who knows—your pet may even get to like it!

keep that ferret odor in check. Bathing your pet once a week in the summer, and once every two weeks in the winter, can help. Some ferrets will take to the water, and some won't. Some will play and swim in it. Other ferrets may be a little fearful at first. In any event, the important

There are three good places to bathe your ferret: the bathtub, under the faucet in the kitchen sink, or better yet in a double basin sink.

If you use the tub, only put enough water in it so that the ferret's feet can touch bottom—about four to five inches deep.

Make sure that the water is not too hot or too cold. Wet the ferret down, then lather him up with a tearless, baby shampoo and give him a good little scrubbing. Then rinse the ferret off completely and take him out of the tub.

Wrap up your pet in a terry cloth towel and dry him well. Make sure that you take him into a draft-free room so he won't catch cold—a common occurrence, especially after a bath in the winter.

Check the ferret's skin to make sure that it's not drying

After shampooing your ferret, be sure to rinse him thoroughly. You must remove all the soap from his coat.

out or flaking. If it is, you might want to cut down on the frequency of shampooing. Maybe, in this case, it would be better to bathe the ferret once every ten days or two weeks in the summer; and maybe once every two-and-one-half weeks in the winter. The ferret's skin is not very porous; it dries out and can be sensitive to detergent. Therefore, be sure to use a very gentle shampoo; you might also want to use a gentle conditioner.

Again, even though some ferrets seem to be swimming like Olympic champions, never leave a ferret alone when he is in the water—always keep an eye on him.

FERRET MANICURE

Another aspect of grooming involves a manicure for your ferret. Ferrets' claws can get very sharp—sharp enough to scratch. While ferrets don't usually destroy furniture, their claws should be clipped frequently. They might greet you at the door and, in their exuberance to see you, accidentally put a little tear into your best outfit.

Use a cat claw clipper to clip a ferret's claws; a regular human nail clipper will do too. The ferret's nail should be clipped just short of the blood vein. The blood vein runs down the middle of the nail. Be especially careful not to cut into

Opposite: Bathing two ferrets at a time is usually not a good idea. One is enough of a handful.

21

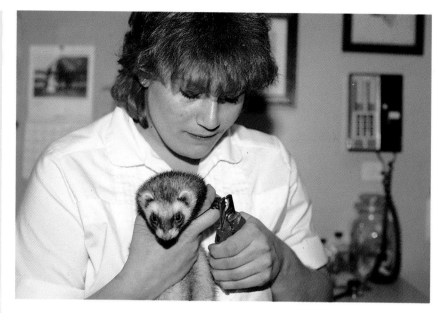

Regular manicuring is a must for your ferret. Use either a cat clipper or one made for humans.

it because it will bleed and cause the animal pain. If you accidentally cut into the vein, or quick, apply styptic powder (available at your local pet shop) to stop the bleeding.

When you are cutting the ferret's nails, turn the nail clipper sideways to avoid cutting into the ferret's toe or any of the tiny pads on the ferret's feet. These tiny, sensitive pads help the animal to locate things. When you are clipping the ferret's nails, only the sharp points should be removed. It might be a good idea to get someone to help you for the first few cuttings—or

until you are comfortable with the ferret, and vice versa! On one of your trips to the vet you may also ask the vet to show you the proper way to clip the ferret's nails, or make the "manicure" part of the ferret's regular visit to the vet.

EAR CARE

The ferret's ears should be checked periodically and cleaned if necessary. This can be done by using cotton swabs dipped in very small amounts of peroxide; or you could ask your veterinarian to suggest other cleaning solutions. Take the cotton swab and gently wipe the

grooming is taking care of the animal's coat. Ferrets will increase their fat layer and grow a thick coat for winter. The winter weight helps to keep the ferret's body temperature at its normal 101.9°F (39°C). After the winter is over, the ferret will lose this layer of body fat and shed its winter coat; this is a good time to brush the ferret, as its lighter coat returns in the spring.

Ferret claws have been known to rip clothes. Therefore, keeping them short is a good idea.

ferret's *outer* ear. The inner ear of any animal is very sensitive, so be sure to go lightly on the ferret's ear.

Ferrets can get ear mites. If you see your ferret scratching his ears a lot, it could indicate that he is being bothered by these pests. A black, waxy build-up is another sign of ear mites. You have a choice: treat the condition yourself by following the directions on an ear mite medication used for cats; or, if you find that you would rather *not* do this, take your pet to the veterinarian.

Another aspect of good

Four Paws Ferret Glow eliminates a ferret's body odor while leaving a lustrous coat.

Housing

If you are like many pet lovers, those little critters that you bring home usually wind up sleeping at the foot of your bed

Note the bell on the collar of this fellow. The bell tells the owner when the ferret is underfoot.

or on a soft, comfortable chair or sofa in your living room. But when you first bring your ferret home you will want to set up some kind of housing for him.

One type of housing that some owners use is an old aquarium. Be sure to put a wire top on the aquarium to prevent the ferret from escaping. You could use some old towels or cotton rags for bedding and place a small dish pan in one corner for the litter pan. The bedding should be changed several times a week. Critics of this type of ferret housing say it is really not the best place for your ferret to live because the litter pan is difficult to clean.

A popular type of housing for the ferret is the wire cage. You could buy or make one with or without a tray. Cages can be constructed from heavy wire mesh that will allow most wastes to fall into pans below it. Or you could put a litter pan in the cage in one corner. Ferrets usually use one area of the cage for these bodily functions.

The cage should also have an enclosed area—maybe a tissue box—where they can snuggle up and rest. You will also want to put a water bottle on the cage. It should also be

mentioned that ferrets have sensitive feet, so don't give them a wiry floor to walk around on. Make it a comfortable surface—not wood, though, because wood absorbs odors—and put down some towels or old rags as bedding.

Ferrets can be either indoor or outdoor pets. If you are planning to keep your ferrets in your backyard, you must provide housing. Introduce the ferrets to the great outdoors toward the end of the summer, after the hot days are over. This way, the ferret will gradually get used to the cooling outdoor temperatures. And when summer rolls around again, make sure that the cage is out of the sun. Summer is the worst season of the year for ferrets. When the temperature gets up there, they can dehydrate very

The ferret cage should be large enough for the animals to move about and stand up comfortably.

Litter pans come in a variety of styles and sizes. When selecting a litter pan, choose one that is sturdy and easy to clean. Photo courtesy Rolf C. Hagen Corp.

quickly and come down with heat prostration. Remember to keep plenty of water outside for them at all times. In the summer, make sure that they don't go swimming or fall asleep in their water bowl.

The indoor ferret is not subject to rabies because it does not come into contact with other animals. But outdoors, the ferret could attract unwelcome visitors. Make sure that the animal's outdoor cage is very secure. It also must be bat-proof, to ensure that the ferret is not exposed to rabies from this creature. The outdoor cage should also be secure against any unwanted visits from

raccoons and possums.

It is okay to leave ferrets outside in the cage in the winter. Their coats are thicker at that time of the year, and they have been putting on an extra layer of body fat since the autumn. But while the winter coat is thick enough to keep the ferret warm, make sure that his cage doesn't get too damp.

Give your ferret a clean, warm house. Wood chips should not be used in a ferret's bedding because they irritate the skin. Sawdust and sand are also bad.

Because the weather is always changing, you might consider making your ferret's outdoor cage a portable one. Then, if it gets too hot in the summer, you can move it to a nice, shady spot. Whatever the season, the cage should have the proper ventilation—to keep the ferret cool in the summer, warm in the winter, and dry in damp weather.

LITTER TRAINING

When you first bring your ferret home it would be best to put him in a temporary cage. A young ferret brought into new surroundings might be skittish or nervous and attempt to run and hide where you might not be able to find him.

Putting him in a temporary

cage will prevent this from happening; it will also make it a lot easier for you to train your new pet. Set up the cage with a small litter pan or a small plastic dish pan. Three sides should be at least three-and-one-half to four inches high, but one side should be cut low to make it easy for the ferret to climb in and out. Ferrets are not known for their climbing ability.

Fill the bottom of the litter pan with about three to four inches of litter; most commercial cat litter brands will be okay. Green litter may be more absorbent than the clay, but if the litter pan is cleaned

Most ferret owners use commercial cat litter in their pets' litter pans. The litter pan should be set up and ready to use before you bring your pet home. Photo courtesy Rolf C. Hagen Corp.

regularly, as it should be, this doesn't really matter. Ferrets back themselves into a corner to defecate and urinate, so be sure that the litter is piled high in those places and that the pan is high enough to prevent accidents. At the beginning of the training period, keep some feces in the pan so your ferret

rest of the cage area is also kept clean during this training period.

If, after a while, you decide to expand the ferret's living space, it might be a good idea to place another litter pan in another part of the house. Watch to make sure that your pet is not relieving himself

Before allowing your ferret to roam the house at will, be sure he is properly litter trained.

doesn't mistake his litter box for some sandbox left there for his amusement. Ferrets are instinctively clean, so you must be sure he understands what the litter pan is intended for; otherwise he may just decide to sleep in the pan and do his toilet business elsewhere. Be sure the

anywhere else. If this happens, you might have to confine him to a small area again and reinforce the correct use of the litter pan. Increase his living space when you feel that he has been completely trained. It is probably best to increase the ferret space one room at a time;

Many ferrets love to play with telephones. It is a good idea to place phones and other small appliances out of reach.

while doing this, be sure that there is a litter pan available for his use.

If you don't intend to put your ferret in a cage, housebreak him in a small room. Since ferrets gravitate to corners, put the litter pan in a corner of the room, again with some feces in it, and the animal should learn to use it correctly.

When you're first litter-training your ferret, you should know that he will usually relieve himself right after he wakes up. This would be a good time to make sure that he is using the litter. One ferret owner makes it a practice to give her pet a treat each time it uses the litter. This greatly helps to reinforce the training.

FERRET-PROOFING THE HOUSE

Pet lovers also like to keep their homes neat and in order. For this reason, they often ask if ferrets scratch, claw, or damage furniture. Ferrets don't usually dig their claws into the upholstery on a couch or a chair the way a cat often does. However, ferrets do like to get into things. If they see a torn cover on a couch, they might take the bottom out, go right through it, and disappear. You've especially got to make sure they don't get caught in your favorite reclining easy-chair either. These chairs can be deadly!

Ferrets often get under the refrigerator or stove; try to block these areas if possible. You should also take steps to keep them from getting into air-conditioning and heating vents. In fact, you've got to be unusually careful with ferrets—they can get into and under most anything because their bodies can flatten out. Washers and dryers, dishwashers, and other appliances should also be ferret-proofed by blocking openings with rolled wire, wood, or other materials.

Watch out for a lump in the rug—it could be a ferret. Ferrets don't usually make loud noises, but if you accidentally step on one you might hear an uncharacteristic scream or two.

Ferrets will chew on electric cords. They have also been known to dig up plants, so don't leave your flora on the floor or within easy reach of the ferret.

Ferrets love to play with toys, but kits and even older ferrets can swallow pieces of rubber. This could be very serious and may require surgery; therefore, watch what they are playing with, and make sure that their toys are still in one piece.

Your pet ferret may enjoy digging up and chewing on potted plants. Before leaving any plant within reach, be sure it is not poisonous. Consult your veterinarian.

Health

DESCENTING

The adult ferret has a natural musky odor that most people of the anal sacs and ducts, which dramatically reduces the objectionable odor.

A healthy ferret will have a clean coat, bright eyes, and a good appetite.

find unpleasant. Bathing can help, but the odor will still be there, and it may linger in your clothing even after you've washed your clothes. The best thing to do is to have the ferret descented. The ferret's odor comes from the anal glands. The veterinarian removes some

For the male ferret, descenting is not enough to control the odor; he has to be castrated as well. The female ferret has a milder odor, but should also, in any event, be spayed—for another very important reason, which we will discuss.

Although it is very convenient to walk into a pet store and buy a young ferret that has already been descented and altered, it is probably much better for you to wait until the ferret is six months of age before having it descented or fixed. Bear in mind that the consumer demand for convenience is prompting many dealers to sell young descented and fixed ferrets. This doesn't mean that you have to buy one; you can still get the ferret and have the surgery done when the animal (male or female) is six months old.

ALTERING

If your ferret has not been neutered or spayed by the time it is six months old, be sure to have it done. Again, as in the case of descenting, breeders have said that surgery for the ferret at the age of six weeks, or before the age of six months, is too young. The ferret is a tough little critter—but not that tough. And putting a young ferret through surgery might be a little too hard on the animal.

Unless you are planning to breed ferrets, there is no reason not to have your animals altered. And in the case of the female ferret it is absolutely imperative that this be done. She will stay in heat for her entire breeding season. If not bred during this time, she will be susceptible to infection and disease which can cause death. Therefore, unless she is being bred, she *must* be spayed. The male ferret, for your own sake and his, should also be castrated. A male that isn't castrated will be much more aggressive and at times will have to be housed separately.

For either the male or female

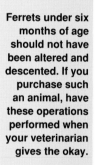

Ferrets under six months of age should not have been altered and descented. If you purchase such an animal, have these operations performed when your veterinarian gives the okay.

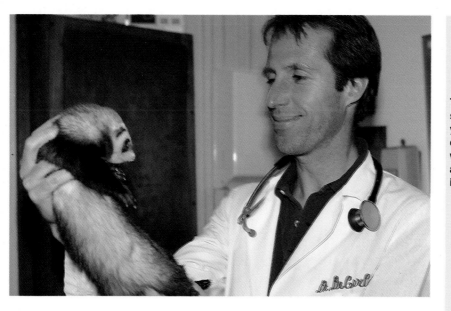

The pet ferret
should receive a
yearly veterinary
check-up which
will include
annual
inoculations.

ferret, wait until they are six months of age before you bring them to your veterinarian for the castrating and/or spaying.

DISTEMPER

Ferrets are very prone to canine (dog) distemper. It is essential that a ferret receive a canine distemper shot. Those exposed to canine distemper for 15 minutes will come down with the deadly disease, and almost 100% of all those contracting it will die.

Young ferrets should get their first vaccine at about eight weeks of age. A booster shot should be given two weeks after that. You might even want to give them shots at eight and ten and 12 weeks of age. The idea behind this is that if the ferret's mother has had her shots, there is a certain amount of immunity provided to the kits. This usually lasts sometime into that eight to 12 week range. When the mother's immunity is protecting the kits, the distemper shots don't take. The idea behind giving the three shots is that somewhere you'll hit the point where the mother's immunity has stopped and the distemper shot will then take.

It is very important that this distemper vaccine not be of

ferret origin. The shot should be a modified live vaccine. It is also recommended that each additional year the animal be given a booster shot to guard against this deadly disease.

Feline distemper is highly contagious among cats and has a high mortality rate. While they are rare, there have been cases of feline distemper in ferrets. It would not hurt to protect your ferret against feline distemper by giving it a feline distemper shot.

RABIES

The subject of rabies shots is a very controversial issue. There is no effective rabies vaccine for ferrets. If one does bite someone, the local health department will probably demand that the animal be sacrificed and examined for rabies.

Some vets simply do not recommend vaccinating ferrets against rabies. But if you decide to have your pet vaccinated for rabies, it is imperative that the veterinarian use a killed virus vaccine—not a modified live vaccine. Not only will the ferret come down with rabies, if a modified live virus is used, but there is the chance that the

disease could be transmitted to humans.

If your pet is kept indoors, the exposure to the rabies virus is minimal. But if you do decide to give the rabies vaccine to your animal, this should not be done before the ferret is six months old.

OTHER HEALTH PROBLEMS

Like people, the ferret can catch cold from time to time. If you have a cold, the ferret can

Have your vet check your pet's ears for ear mites and other parasites.

even get it from you. Sometimes the cold comes from being in a drafty room, especially after one of the ferret's weekly summer or every-other-week winter baths. You'll know if the ferret has a cold because its nose will be runny; it will be sneezing; and the animal may even run a temperature. Of course, it is best to try to avoid getting a cold. Make sure you dry the ferret thoroughly after the bath. Also see to it that your pet is kept in a warm, dry place. Make sure that his bowl of water doesn't spill over onto his bedding.

Stomach problems also occur if the ferret has eaten something that has disagreed with it. Usually, something like milk or meat can cause diarrhea; if the ferret has it, don't give him any more milk or meat for a few days. As with humans, when the stomach's upset it may be better to go easy on food for a while. Diarrhea should go away in a day or two; if it persists longer, it's time to call the veterinarian.

Ferrets are bothered from time to time by fleas and ear mites. Fleas are sometimes eliminated by using the same kind of flea dip used to get rid of fleas in cats. Fleas also get into the carpet and even furniture. There are products on the market that you can use to spray these places. As with cats, if flea infestation becomes too great you may have to call an exterminator to have your house "bombed."

While ferrets don't get worms the way cats and dogs do, they are sometimes bothered by heartworms. Heartworms are spread by mosquitoes and are a natural parasite of dogs. Heartworms are usually fatal to the ferret on the rare occasions when there is an outbreak. The best thing to do in this case is to give the ferret the same

As you become acquainted with your new pet, you will recognize his regular, healthy behavior.

The ferret on the left is healthy, while that on the right suffers from coccidiosis, a serious ailment among ferrets.

condition should think about breeding. And, of course, if she isn't spayed she is susceptible to infection and death.

Ferrets do not have great vision to begin with; on top of this, they can get cataracts. Don't confuse the two; but if you think that there is something wrong with the ferret's eyes, take it to your veterinarian. Less serious eye problems, like watery eyes, can be cleared up with medication.

FIRST AID FOR FERRETS

Like people, pets need first aid on those hopefully rare occasions when they are injured either by people or other animals; or, in the case of the ferret, by the things they get into because of their inquisitive nature. Ferret-proofing your house—and even your car—is the first step to take to prevent your pet from getting hurt.

It is not a good idea to let your ferret loose in the car while you are driving; but if you do allow the ferret to be loose in your car, make sure that there are no openings—in the seats, on the floor, on the car door, or even on the dashboard—for the ferret to slip through. A ferret can easily get caught in a car

preventive medicine, at a much lower dosage, that you would give a dog in high-risk areas. (Consult your vet first!) The use of indoor housing or mosquito netting on outdoor cages also helps to minimize this kind of disease.

The pregnant ferret is prone to all kinds of illness, which is one reason why only those that are truly committed to taking care of the animal and assuming all the responsibilities of her door; accidentally slamming it on the animal would be quite a shock for the ferret's slight body. It may *look* okay after it's been caught in one of these unfortunate mishaps, but the ferret could have been seriously injured internally. It would be wise to take the animal to the veterinarian to have him checked over to make sure that nothing is seriously wrong.

Ferret owners say that another common accident to watch out for, and prevent from happening, is the ferret getting stuck inside a reclining chair or hide-away sofa. Here again, the ferret could be crushed by the impact of all that weight— including yours! Also be sure to avoid accidentally stepping on the ferret that might be sleeping under a rug. If you or someone else should step on your ferret, the animal's back could be broken. If you notice that the ferret is *not* moving around the way he or she normally moves, take him to your veterinarian immediately.

Ferrets have been known to scurry about the kitchen and suffer minor or major burns from accidental contact with toasters, stoves, ovens, and other appliances. If the ferret does get burned, apply ice to the injury. If the animal seems to have been burned seriously, take him to the veterinarian.

Kitchens are also stocked these days with boxes and containers of chemical cleaning solutions—which someone may have forgotten to secure. If your ferret gets an accidental dose of any toxic chemical, *rush* him to the veterinarian and bring along whatever it was that he ingested.

When domestic animals are playing, and ferrets will kid around with anything, they are usually doing just that— playing. But if one of the animals accidentally (or otherwise!) takes a chunk out of

Before adding a new ferret to others in your menagerie, quarantine him for a few weeks to see that all is well.

Keep all electrical cords out of reach of your ferret to prevent electrocution.

the other animal, make sure that the bite wound isn't serious. If there is a significant amount of bleeding or if the cut looks bad, call the veterinarian. If the ferret has been bitten by an outdoor animal, like a raccoon for instance, take him to the veterinarian immediately.

You should check your ferret's stool periodically for any irregularities. The stool is an indication of poor or good health in your pet.

If the ferret has diarrhea it may have something to do with the diet you are feeding him. Diarrhea is often caused by products containing milk.

Eliminate milk products first. Diarrhea can also be brought about by a change in your ferret's diet. You might consider returning to what you were feeding your ferret previously if there was no adverse reaction to it. Diarrhea lasting for more than a few days can be serious; ferrets can become dehydrated. Take your pet to the veterinarian, who should be able to stabilize this stomach disorder. An absence of stool for more than 24 hours should not be ignored. This may indicate a blockage of some kind. The ferret should be taken to the veterinarian, who will locate the cause. If there is one, surgery may be necessary in order to remove the blockage.

Except for the initial stool after whelping, black tarry stools can be signs of internal bleeding. There may be an infection in the intestinal tract. It may also indicate stress. Regardless, this condition should be treated by your veterinarian. Ferrets are small animals and most illnesses need to be taken seriously. Vomiting, although rare in the ferret, may be a sign of an intestinal virus which may disappear in a few days. Vomiting and no stool for 24 hours, however, could be an indication of a more serious condition. There may be a blockage, and once again surgery may be required. You and the ferret simply cannot afford to wait.

VETERINARY CARE

Because ferrets are not as common around the house (or anywhere else for that matter) as cats and dogs, even veterinarians are still learning about them. Although most veterinarians are qualified to treat ferrets, it's probably best to go to one who has been recommended by a ferret owner. Oftentimes, the representative of a local ferret club can provide the name of a good vet "who knows what he's doing" when it comes to treating these animals.

Ferrets should usually see the veterinarian once a year, for a canine distemper shot and a check-up.

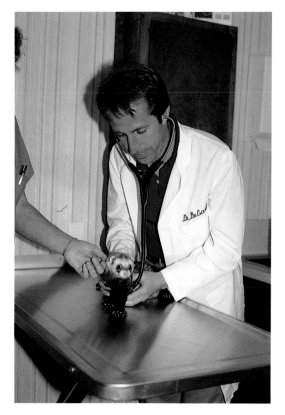

The best rule of thumb for your pet's health is this: if in doubt, see the vet.

Ferret Reproductive System

The ferret reproductive system is very different from that of a cat or a dog. They are seasonal breeders, which means

Before breeding your ferret, think about the enormous responsibility involved.

A litter of three-week-old ferret kits.

that they reproduce only during a certain time of the year (usually from March to August) in a natural environment. Mother Nature seems to have lent the ferret a helping hand because the young ferrets (kits) are born only in the spring and in the summer, the times of the year when the weather is warmer and when it is easier to get food and water, thus much easier to stay alive.

The ferret usually becomes sexually mature the first spring after it is born. The female ferret mates only when she is in heat. At other times she will refuse the male ferret and will not become pregnant. The male ferret's season starts a little earlier, but while he is waiting for the female to go into heat, his body is readying itself.

Ferrets are turned on by light—literally. The ferret's yearly cycle of sexual activity is regulated by light; as spring approaches, the days start getting longer and the nights shorter. This change in the length of the day (the increased amount of daylight) is picked up by the ferret's eyes and signals are sent to the brain, which then activates the sexual process.

Using the length of daylight to control the ferret's reproductive behavior is good for the ferret because if another element, such as temperature, were used to signal the sexual activity, it could mislead the animal. Unseasonably warm weather in the winter could confuse matters, disrupting the timing and causing the young ferrets to be born too early in the year, or too late.

testicles will enlarge. Both sexes will emit a strong body odor. The male will mark his territory by spraying. Mating takes ten minutes to several hours. After this breeding—which can be violent (the male dragging the female around by the scruff of the neck until she is limp)—the female's swollen vulva will shrink back to its normal size or close to it within two to two-and-a-half weeks. If it doesn't, the female ferret should be re-mated.

PREGNANCY

After the female is bred, it will be about a week to ten days before you know whether or not she is pregnant. If she is pregnant, one of the only signs at this time will be the decrease in the size of her vulva. It may not go completely down to normal size but it will be considerably smaller. There may be a slight discharge from the vulva at this time. This is nothing to be alarmed about as long as the discharge is clear. If it is a colored discharge, take her to the veterinarian for medication.

Pregnancy lasts about 42 days. The female ferret will be her usual self up until the last

The average ferret litter will contain six or seven kits. Litters as large as 13 have occured.

It has been said that because ferrets respond to light, you could use artificial indoor lighting to simulate the change in the seasons and bring the ferret into prime. But it's probably a better idea to let Mother Nature run the show.

When the female goes into heat, the uterus is enlarged and there is an increase in the amount of fluids secreted. The vulva swells up enormously. The female ferret, however, will not make the kinds of noises made by the cat in heat.

As for the male ferret, during the breeding season, the

week or so of her pregnancy. Her appetite may increase slightly so be sure she has enough food. This food should be high quality so she doesn't get fat. She may also be less active at this time and sleep more. Her last two weeks of pregnancy should be spent in the place where she will be find her.

If your ferret is confined to her cage that last week, make sure it is equipped with a nesting box that has some sort of soft bedding. A terry cloth towel or soft cloth would be good. The sides of the box should be low enough for her to climb into and out of easily,

Ferret kits are usually weaned in about six or seven weeks, when their personalities begin to emerge.

having her kits; this way she will be used to her confined area by the time the kits are born. Do not confine her at the last minute, because she may find this upsetting. Although you may not be needed during the delivery, you should stay close by; but if the ferret has not been confined to a particular area, you may not be able to without the possibility of overturning it.

Your animal will probably want her privacy during the birth of her kits, but you should be close in case you're needed for some reason. Most likely the delivery will proceed without incident, but if you see that the ferret is having difficulty and is unable to deliver her kits, take

All ferrets, like all people, have highly individual personalities.

her to the vet.

Once the kits are born it is normal for the mother to be protective of her babies and not want them handled just yet. When she lets you know it's okay to handle them, proceed with caution and care.

The kits may be born anywhere from minutes to hours apart. And there may be as few as one or as many as 13 kits with the average litter size being about six or seven. New kits weigh about five grams and grow rapidly. They are usually weaned at around six to eight weeks, depending on their size.

Gradually introduce into their diet some dry cat food thoroughly moistened with water. Place it in the cage with the ferret and kits. This will make them a little less dependent on their mother and get them used to the food.

An important thing to remember at this time is that once the ferrets reach three weeks of age they should be handled by you. Start picking them up gently and talking to them and playing carefully with them. Ferrets that have been handled usually make the friendliest pets.

Always remember that if you own a female ferret who comes into heat, she must be bred or spayed. If not bred, the jill (female) will remain in heat for three to four months and become susceptible to septicemia resulting in death. This is due to the enlarged vulva which becomes a breeding ground for bacteria and infection. She may also contract aplastic anemia, which can also cause death.

Unless you are planning to breed ferrets it is best to have the female spayed before she goes into her first heat.

For those who think that it might be a good idea to breed ferrets, it should be added that there is an enormous responsibility involved; little of this may be anticipated by the casual breeder. One ferret owner told the president of a local ferret association that she was going to breed her ferrets. The president of the ferret organization asked her, "What are you going to do with them?" The prospective ferret breeder said, "Sell them." A few weeks later, this same ferret breeder called the president of the ferret group back and said, "I have a litter; what do I do with them now?"

Again, leave the ferret breeding to the professionals, or to those who are strongly committed to taking on all of the responsibilities that go along with this work.

Another note on the ferret's reproductive activity: ferrets can go through what is called "false pregnancy." When this happens, the female ferret will swell up just as if she were pregnant—but 42 days later there are no kits. If your female ferret goes through a false pregnancy, she may even start acting like a mother at the end of the 42-day gestation period. Because she has no kits, she may adopt anyone in sight—even you!

Breeders must separate ferrets during the breeding season. Males who are in season are aggressive, hostile, and capable of killing other ferrets. Don't put two male ferrets together in the same cage or they will kill each other when they are in season.

FERRETS AND CHILDREN

One of the frequent attacks made on ferrets by their enemies—whether people or government bodies—is that they pose a real danger to children. There are, government agencies say, "documented attacks" on small children by ferrets; they seem to take this to mean that the ferret should be outlawed because of it. Well,

All children should be made aware of the responsibilities of ferret ownership before being left alone with the animals.

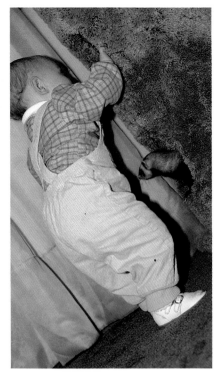

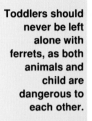

Toddlers should never be left alone with ferrets, as both animals and child are dangerous to each other.

good idea to keep an eye on children under the age of nine when they are in the company of pet animals. You simply don't leave a two-year-old alone in the same room with a ferret—or with a German Shepherd or a Siamese cat. The key word here is supervision. Adults have to watch children when pets are around.

Some of the incidents of ferret "attack" point to an adult who is not thinking. There was the case of a woman who took her baby into a pet store and put its face up to the ferret cage. The ferret bit the kid's nose. Said one ferret owner, "You really have to know your ferrets. It's like a cat or a dog. It really makes me nervous to see people buy a ferret and put it right up to their neck. Ferrets like to bite chins. You really have to know your ferrets."

What people should also know is that ferrets might not be the best pet for small children. Unless you are willing to assume the responsibility of watching the active ferret and the active toddler at the same time, you should wait until children are a little older before bringing a ferret into your home.

say ferret lovers, there are "documented attacks" on small children by other animals, too, but this hasn't prompted government agencies to try to eliminate these animals as household pets.

In many cases, what's really at the heart of all this is good old common sense, or a lack of it on the part of people who leave children, particularly toddlers, alone with animals. Depending on the child's maturity, which is a very relative thing, it is always a

Ferrets and Other Pets

Ferrets get along with other animals, but common sense

ferrets playing hide-and-seek with a German Shepherd. The

Ferrets can make friends with other animals if they are properly acquainted under supervised conditions.

dictates that if you *do* have other animals and are bringing a ferret home for the first time, gradually introduce them to one another. Ferrets are adaptable and will most likely, in time, get along with your other animals. They may even become good friends. Ferrets have been known to teach other animals ferret games. We witnessed

ferrets were running in and out of a makeshift tunnel while the dog was waiting at the end of the tubing for them. And they all seemed to be having a lot of fun.

Give your animals time to get to know one another. Don't put them together the first day and leave them alone. In fact, it might take some time before

Albino ferret listening to some tunes.

you'd want to leave them unattended. Let them stay together for short periods at first. Gradually increase the time they spend together until they seem to be totally comfortable around each other. But even at this point, it might not be a good idea to leave them without your supervision. Use your judgment. You will probably be able to tell when the time comes that you can trust all the animals alone together.

While cats, dogs, and ferrets can become good friends, you might want to keep your ferret away from parrots and other birds.

People out shopping for ferrets have been told that they have to come from the same litter to get along. There is no reason for this to be true. You can also put an older ferret in with a younger one. Just allow the same rules to apply—give them time to get to know one another. The animals stay playful throughout most of their lives and would probably appreciate another ferret for company. We say *probably*— there's that rare ferret who prefers being an "only ferret," no doubt.

If we could even go so far as to make a suggestion, perhaps you should consider getting two ferrets.

Travelling with Your Ferret

The best way to transport a ferret is in a case of some kind.

length of time—while you're shopping, for example.

Note the leash on this ferret. If you allow your ferret to roam freely outdoors, chances are he'll disappear down the first interesting burrow he sees.

A cat carrier will do. If you're driving, it's much better not to let the ferret loose in the car, even if it seems to be comfortably nestled on your lap or on the seat. Keep ferrets in carriers in the car.

And don't, of course, leave your pet alone in the car for any

Especially avoid doing so on a warm day. Ferrets dehydrate quickly. A wise practice is to play it safe by taking along a water bottle. If you're going to the park, or the beach (one of the ferret's favorite stomping grounds), take a leash.

Ferrets usually enjoy going

Allowing your ferret some time to look around a new place will help allay his curiosity—he may even get bored after a while.

places and are easy to take along. Once you get to your destination, your pet can be carried around in your arms or a large carrying bag.

WHEN YOU TRAVEL

When you are going away, say on your vacation, and you are not taking your ferret with you, what do you do with it? It is not a good idea to put the ferret in a boarding kennel, say many ferret owners. There are too many possible ferret health hazards. The best thing to do if you are going away is to have a reliable friend ("reliable" is important) take care of your pet for you, either in your home or in his. It's also better to let someone who has a way with animals take care of him—and it's probably better still to leave your ferret with someone who knows about all the different ways ferrets can get into mischief. If your house has been ferret-proofed (openings blocked so the animal can't get into refrigerators, stoves, air-conditioning, or heating vents) the friend who is watching your ferret should also take the same precautions.

You could also let the ferret sitter know what your pet likes to eat. Remind him/her that ferrets need plenty of water and that they must not be outside. Give the sitter the name of your veterinarian in case of emergency as well as the number where you can be reached if necessary.

Colors

Do you like a cute little animal that looks a little like a raccoon? Well, the sable colored ferret might be for you.

A trio of ferrets. Ferrets come in several different colors and coat and body types. There is something for everyone.

It is the most common and the most popular. The coat will range from dark to light brown. The undercoat will go from white or cream to beige. Sables that are clearly marked will have a very definite mask.

The albino is also a popular color. We say color, but the coat of the albino ferret, which appears to be white, is technically colorless. Ferret fanciers who enter their albinos in shows strive for the whitest coat possible, but most albino ferrets have a slight tint to their fur that is creamy or yellowish. During mating season some albino ferrets can actually develop a golden tint. Sunlight will also react with this ferret's body oils to produce tints in the

It is difficult, if not impossible, to gauge the quality of the ferret's coat color before maturity.

fur. Their coat is somewhat longer and more coarse. Although most albinos are red-eyed, breeders have also developed a black-eyed white variety.

Silver-mitt ferrets sport white feet or legs and often a white patch on the neck. Silver-mitts range from beige to dark brown. The combination of black and white guard hairs gives them that silvery coloration.

Silver ferrets are similar in marking to the silver-mitt, except that they have more white in the guard hair, giving them a lighter silvery look.

The Siamese ferret has coloring similar to that of the Siamese cat. Its coat is brown with underfur that's beige to cream. Its points (ears, feet, tail, and nose) should all be the same color, usually brown. The Siamese ferret's richly colored markings deepen with age.

Other colors for the ferret include butterscotch and cinnamon.

Of course, the color of the ferret has no bearing on its individual personality. Also keep in mind that kits do not develop their masks for a while, so don't expect to find a kit with that perfect bandit-like mask.

SHOW FERRETS

Shows are becoming more and more popular with ferret enthusiasts. The goal of a show is to find the ideal, or "perfect," ferret. There usually are several categories in the show competition and two basic ferret types. The bulldog is a sturdy-looking ferret, with short, thick legs and neck. The whippet type is just the opposite—a thin-boned, lanky-looking ferret with more pointed features than the blunt-looking bulldog. Between these two extreme body types is the average body type. The ideal for all three types in show competition is to look healthy, strong, and well shaped. The actual weight is not so important so long as the animal on its skin, or any mutations. You would, of course, also want to make sure that its claws are trimmed.

The ferret that you are entering in a show should have a tail that in no way resembles the tail of a rat. His coat should also be thick and soft—and clean!

Naturally, you would never

If you plan on showing your ferrets in competition, they must be squeaky clean. Don't let them romp in the mud the day before!

is in top physical condition—the ferret should be fit, not fat.

The ferret has 40 teeth; teeth are usually a sign of an animal's condition. The show ferret should have a full set of teeth which should be clean and white.

If you're thinking of entering your pet in a ferret show, you should make sure that the animal has no unusual bumps enter in a show a ferret that has any type of parasites. The show animal must also be in good health at the time of the show—no runny nose or watery eyes. And no ferret will win a show competition or even get a chance to enter one if any body parts have been either surgically removed (the only surgical alterations permitted are those for descenting and altering) or lost in an accident.

The ideal show ferret should not be jumpy. Its disposition should be steady and its demeanor friendly. The show ferret should be relaxed—he or she *must* be relaxed with all those other people there, not to mention all those other ferrets.

The albino ferret has been a prize winner over the years. But it may take a little extra work for you to keep its fur nice and white. Show albinos have to be bathed about twice a week; no colors, artificial or otherwise, should be used to help "gussy up" the show ferret. With the exception of pet shampoo, the use of any kind of chemical coloring or chemical process on the ferret will result in you and your ferret being disqualified from the show.

The ideal albino ferret, it might be added, should look slightly "feline" (like a cat) without any resemblance to the cat's arch-enemy—the rat.

A show ferret must be clean, healthy, alert, and of a nice even temperament.

History

The ferret, *Mustela putorius furo,* is a domesticated ancestor of the ferret is believed to be the polecat. The domestic

A wild polecat, ancestor of today's domesticated ferret.

carnivore belonging to the Mustelidae family. The ferret family includes weasels, minks, ermines, badgers, skunks, sables, and otters. The earliest ferret is not the same as the black-footed ferret, *Mustela nigripes*, which lives in the American West.

The ferret was domesticated

55

Today's ferrets are thoroughly domesticated animals that rely on their human caretakers.

around 3000 BC by the Egyptians, who kept it as a household pet and a rodent controller. The ferret was already established as a household pet and rodent controller in ancient Greece and Rome when the cat was introduced there.

Queen Victoria of England bred white-furred, pink-eyed albino ferrets to give as gifts to her friends among the nobility in the 19th century. Historians also say that Genghis Khan, in the 13th century, had an albino ferret for a pet.

Ferrets have been used throughout history to perform a function known as flushing out rabbits. In the first century AD, a Greek geographer, Strabo, wrote about a plague of rabbits in the Balearic Islands. According to Frederick Zuener's *Domesticated Animals,* this was taken care of by muzzled ferrets which were sent into the rabbit holes. The purpose of the muzzle was to prevent the ferret from making a kill, feasting on it and then staying in the burrow. The only way to recover the animal would have been to dig it out. With the ferret muzzled, however, the rabbits were driven out and caught in a net placed over the exit from the burrow. Little known in America (where it is illegal today), ferreting for rabbits has been practiced for centuries in Europe and Asia.

BLACK-FOOTED FERRET

The domesticated ferret is an entirely different creature than the black-footed ferret, *Mustela nigripes.* Because of his way of life, the black-footed ferret is almost extinct. Feeding mostly on prairie dogs, this animal lives in the American West, in tunnels and dens of the prairie dogs. The prairie dog is a pest for the farmer because he competes with livestock for grazing land and eats farm crops. In order to reduce the prairie dog population, a poison control program was started which had a devastating effect on the black-footed ferret population. The ferrets ate the chemically poisoned prairie and then the ferret itself. Sylvatic plague, the disease that causes bubonic plague in humans, struck Wyoming towns, killing off a large portion of prairie dogs. Just after this disease was brought under control by U.S. wildlife officials, an epidemic of canine

A pet ferret that is let loose to survive in the wilds probably won't survive.

dogs and died in great numbers. For a while it appeared that the black-footed ferret might become extinct.

In 1984, wildlife biologists were sure that the black-footed ferret had made a comeback— 128 had been seen roaming freely in prairie dog towns in Wyoming. But then epidemics killed off the ferret's principal food source—the prairie dog— distemper broke out, virtually destroying the remaining ferret population. Faced with the impending demise of the black-footed ferret, U.S. wildlife officials, in September 1986, decided to bring the last surviving wild members of this endangered breed into a captive-breeding program. A recent head count indicated that there were only 21 of these ferrets left—including the six captured as part of the Wyoming Game and Fish Department's captive-breeding program. However, with the others available for this breeding program, it is hoped that these ferrets will breed well in captivity.

The black-footed ferret resembles the domesticated ferret in size. It has a long body and legs and black tail-tip.

FERRET LAWS

For such a little guy, the ferret is the target of a lot of critical attacks. Ferret critics at times seem to be going after the ferret as though it was a cougar, instead of the small, playful, friendly, domesticated creature that it has been for thousands of years throughout the civilized

Despite the ferret's long history as a domesticated pet, many lawmakers continue to treat it as a wild animal.

with short legs, a sharp-pointed muzzle, small ears and a short tail. Up to two feet in length, including a six-inch tail, it weighs one-and-one-half pounds, the female being smaller than the male. The coat is yellowish-buff with a black band across the eyes, black feet

world.

On behalf of the animal, ferret owners and supporters say that their furry friends are perfect pets: intelligent, playful, affectionate, harmless. They say that ferrets are domestic, not wild, animals who actually need people in order to survive.

In some areas, ferrets are illegal and may be confiscated by agents of the law.

Many of them say that ferrets are safer and a lot less trouble than many dogs. Experts from various fields (biology, mammalogy, veterinary medicine) tend to support this position, agreeing that the ferret is suitable as a domestic pet. And public officials in most states agree. But foes of the ferret say it is a vicious carrier of disease and that if it gets out into the farming communities it will form colonies and destroy agricultural products.

Officials from the U.S. Humane Society and one particular committee from the American Veterinary Medical Association go on to say that they are against ferrets because they cause disease, and because

they will increase too dramatically in population for society to be able to accommodate them. These and others are trying to discourage people from acquiring ferrets as pets.

These vast differences of opinion have produced a variety of legal situations regarding ferrets in the United States today. In the majority of states, people are free to keep pet ferrets. But laws vary, and it would be advisable to check with local health authorities to learn what the legal status of the ferret is in the area where you live. It can become confusing. In some states, like New York State, it is still legal to keep them as pets while in New York

Most experts agree that pet ferrets are less likely to carry rabies than pet dogs and cats.

City it is not. Some states banning ferrets include New Hampshire, Massachusetts, Rhode Island, and California. There has also been recent talk about movements to ban ferrets in West Virginia, Arizona, North Carolina, and Connecticut.

What can you do to help the ferrets' cause—and your own, if you are a ferret-owner? Ferrets do have a friend in Washington; the Pet Industry Joint Advisory Council is one group that is fighting for the rights of the ferret and ferret owner.

The International Ferret Association, the world's largest ferret organization, is also helping ferret-owners pull together to save the ferret as a domestic pet. The International Ferret Association, headquartered in Roanoke, Virginia, and the Pet Industry Joint Advisory Council are there to help if there are any critical attacks on the ferret that you might notice in the local press or issued by local government bodies. Each group urges you to contact them with the details of any misinformation about the ferret that you notice.

Explaining some of the biggest problems that ferrets and ferret owners are facing these days is George Harmon,

Opposite: As the ferret becomes more and more popular as a pet, it seems likely that lawmakers will learn to treat it as such.

executive director of the International Ferret Association. "It seems that again this year," he says, "the leader of the pack against ferrets is the Humane Society of the United States, The Public Health Department, and a number of veterinarians and committees, along with the quickly." There actually have been cases where the state has come in and demanded ferrets from their owners. California, where there are about one million ferrets and 500,000 ferret owners, has been especially demanding.

In California, ferrets are

Albino ferret nosing around the top of its cage.

same jerks from last year, all saying the same thing—that ferrets are a wild animal that bite and attack babies, and all the rest of the same old hogwash."

"It may also be a good idea," he adds, "to set up a safe-house where ferrets can be moved classified by state agencies as "wild animals" and state officials will confiscate your ferret. But people are starting to assert their rights to have ferrets, and they are also trying to reason with these state agencies in order to establish a more "humane" way of addressing the ownership of pet ferrets.

The main point of contention in the state of California is the "wild animal" classification. Hundreds of reference books refer to the ferret as a "domestic animal," and eventually the state of California and other states may learn what the ferret is really like, if the ferret owners and enthusiasts keep up their work to educate state officials responsible for this deplorable state of affairs for the ferret.

The best ferret owner is an informed ferret owner.

What do you do if you live in an area where ferret ownership is banned? In most cases, you will still be able to get veterinary care for the ferret, if it is needed. As for legal trouble, you would, of course, want to avoid that at all costs. By keeping your ferret in your home, away from young children, you should be able to make the best of this situation, even when the law is not working for you.

All in all, there has been a lot of misleading information going around about the ferret—and it is often issued by government agencies. The chief fallacy is the public description of the ferret as a wild animal. Efforts are now underway by ferret organizations and ferret owners throughout the United States to clear up this misunderstanding and to protect the pet ferret.

Index